Forex Trading

Amazing Basic Guide for Beginners Get First Profitable Victory and More

© Copyright 2018 by Noah Gladwyn -All rights reserved.

Author reserve all rights to this document. No one is allowed to print, reproduce, copy or mimic any of the passage of this document without written permission of the author. Reviewers are allowed to quote a few lines in the reviews.

Disclaimer

No section, line or paragraph of the publication must be reproduced and transmitted by mechanical, electronic or handwriting mean, such as photocopy, recording or any other system without permission in writing from author and publisher.

The purpose of this document is to share verified information, but the author and publisher will not assume any liability for errors, omission and opposing interoperations of the content herein.

The purpose of this book is entertainment and the views and ideas in the book only belong to the author. These ideas should not be taken as expert advice and commands. The readers are only responsible for their actions for doing anything wrong after reading this book.

Only purchaser and reader are responsible to adhere to the application of laws and regulations in their state for advertising, professional licensing and business practices.

Neither author nor the publisher will assume responsibility or liability for actions of purchaser or reader. All brands and trademarks in this book are for clarification purposes and owned by the owners only. They are not affiliated with the document.

Table of Content

Introduction..5

Chapter 1: What is exactly forex trading? And why is it interesting?... 6

Chapter 2: Mindset and Psychology for forex trading...............10

Chapter 3: Keeping track of forex trading and protect own information... 14

Chapter 4: Making the perfect plan to trade............................ 28

Chapter 5: Tools for mastering forex trading........................... 34

Chapter 6: Choosing currencies to trade...................................39

Chapter 7: Common terminologies in forex trading..................44

Chapter 8: Traits of successful forex traders........................... 45

Conclusion... 48

Introduction

Financial world is always the big and interesting topics to a large of population nowadays because it effects in may aspects of life. The currencies are the big part of that.

Forex trading are the words you hear a lot of times if you turn on or accidentally stumble on the financial news channel. Forex is the short and simple way of foreign exchange, in here it means not other than currencies. The most obviously evident about forex is when we and our family go travel to another country, we need the currency of that country so we can buy stuff and pay for services when we are there. It is interesting, isn't it?

Chapter 1: What is exactly forex trading? And why is it interesting?

Forex is foreign exchange with the currencies between different countries depend on the rate also. That is why forex trading has another name that is currency trading. Forex trading is the way of purchasing and selling foreign currencies in couple or more with the accepted price. The traders and investors will see this with the their opening eyes.

The world economy is immense with opportunities. Forex trading is one of big the portion of it. The market of forex trading aka currency trading is reaching to more than $5 trillion. With the trillion dollars, everyone will be happy to have a small portion of this huge pie.

Most of companies in the global economy have their shares or stocks to sell to the traders and investors. Here is come the important of the currency in each country. That is why understand about forex trading is crucial.

With the global economy and more and more countries do trade and business with each other. The currencies have to follow as well. Business between countries to countries have to have a observation and understanding about the currencies around the world. One mistake when trading in foreign business can cause big loss and very hard to recover.

As the business owners and traders, we can really profit about the value changing of the currencies around the world. However, we have the right methods and understand them comprehensively from the bottom to the top. That is really an exciting challenge and worth to spend time to achieve.

Forex trading is close with us every single day without we even recognize it. Everyday we earn and spend money. We hear different type of currencies such as US dollar, British pound, Euro, Japanese Yen and so on. The forex trading and its markets are really close to close to many household than we think.

The forex or foreign exchange will never go away instead it will be become bigger and bigger because the needs of trading and paying for the business and services between countries in global economy this century.

Most basic concept of forex trading is the traders buy the currency with is on the slow value trend and sell the currency when it is on the high value trend so the traders will make the profit. It has to be with the pair currencies. That is really easy say than done because a lot of factors will be involve in the trade and analysis.

The factors will be really vast such as inflation, political stability, interest rate, economic performance and much more.

We are sure that all of these factors will always have the big impact on the value of the currencies between countries.

When we buy a currency, we expect it will get higher and more value so when we sell them we can get more and continue to doing that. The pair of currency is really important because we use the currency to purchase another currency.

The terms "appreciation" and "depreciation" are really common in forex trading. They are the one of the reasons why forex is really attract the traders and investors. "Appreciation" is we buy the currency when it was low value and we predict it will increase the value appreciation over time and we make a gain when we sell it. "Depreciation" is we sold our currency with higher price and then when it depreciate value, we buy it back with the cheaper price and we get more of that currency which we want.

The gain is huge if we consider the factors and see it. Currency which we buy low now we can sell it high, and our currency when it drops we can buy it with lower price and get more of them in our portfolio.

Forex trading is happening on the weekdays and through 24 hours. Nonstop on the working weekdays with the interesting analysis to capture this huge liquidity market. Also forex trading has no commission fee. A lot of investments have commission fees that make investors really are hesitated to jump in.

The famous centers or exchanging in the world such as London Exchange, New York Exchange and Tokyo Exchange. A lot of trader really aware and do big transactions on these centers. The currencies are flowing in these centers, and their reputation are stable.

Many people think United States is the biggest market for forex trading. However, the biggest one actually is the United Kingdom. United Kingdom is more than double percent 41% comparing to the United States 19%.

Chapter 2: Mindset and Psychology for forex trading

Is the mindset or psychology important when come to trading? The answer is yes. It is really important. When trading, we will see the different times between gain and loss. That is really a real test with our mind.

Sometimes the loss happened but our mindset need to trust the process and the profitable habit will come. The mindset needs to be right to either to start or continue not even talk about hug success yet. The mindset is important because it is the real reason a lot of new traders gave up.

Many people think that the signals, formulas and indicators will the only ways to lead to success. That is just part true. However, if the mindset not flow and believe to adapt that we will make money. It will become the big obstacle in the future of trading.

Trader believe that will recover the loss

Traders with the strong believe will get back the money that they lost by attach the emotion in the trade and it will be always hard for them to admit the lost cannot be recover. They keep ditch in the hole instead of relying on the facts with right indicators and moving on. The fear of failure is bigger than admit the loss. The fear of failure will be sure lead to the failure path.

In this case, checking the mindset and psychology is so important because the indicators of the mindset will give a clear pictures of what we do wrongly and give a critical decision to be better.

Right expectations at the beginning

We need to have the real goal in mind like how much money we have in our account to start trading, and how much we want to gain the profit and also in how long. These expectations need to be really clear and realistic. Writing them down to the paper or note will help a lot.

The long run will pay this off big time. We can see the example here. If we have $1,000 in the account and expect we will trade here and there for 30 days then get $1,000,000. It will be really big chance that we give up after the month is over. The goal is really unrealistic.

Rich quick

This mindset is the perfect dream for any investor and trader in the financial investment. This is not the right mindset and need to be get rid of before start trading. When the trader want to get rich quick, the trader need to spend more capital to trade. However, there is the no real co relation between put more money in will get more money out in trading.

Many factors and indicators are considered to have the successful trade. When traders just throw the money to trade with no strategies and hope will get it back ten fold, it just like gambling which the risk will be really high. This mindset need to be eliminated.

Traders should treat forex like a real profession. It will need a lot of time and effort to understand and exercise the trade. The knowledge and the strategy are really needed to comprehend the subject.

Forex trading skills will be slow and take time to capture. Our dedications are the key to master the skills. The small profit by time will accumulate and take the trader to the big profit. No way to shortcut and get rick quick.

Set apart money just for trading

We should have the separate money just for trading. It means we will not have to touch on this money for our daily routines, shopping. Some people use their money for shopping, foods, paying debt and so on for the trading. It is really dangerous because now they will be more worried. The mindset will not be clear for the important decision. The good way if we do not have the separate money to trade, just stop all of the activity of trading. We should keep the plan until we have the money.

Value yourself in trading even encountering difficulties or failures

When you first start to trade, even you learn and remember all of the tips and techniques. It will be the chance that you make a mistake or a loss in the trade. That is the process of learning a new skill. When the failure happen, we usually discourage in ourselves. That is just the natural react of human being. Instead of discourage, we can see that like the learning curve experience that analyze with the information what went wrong. We can modify that better next time.

Next trade is completely new trade

When the trade was end, it completely the past trade. When new trade comes up, this is completely different trade. It will not related to the last trade especially about the emotional. Two situations that will often happen are the traders feel very confident or they feel very about I need to win it back mindset from the last trade. They will continue to attach to the previous outcomes. For example, if they win the last 5 trades with the profit, that is not mean to assume that the next 5 trades will be the same.

Chapter 3: Keeping track of forex trading and protect own information

The clear and understanding journal is always the good way to keep track for any trader. However, many of traders completely ignore the important of the journal. At the end of the day, forex trading is not a hobby, it is a real business. It can make a lot of profit if you treat it such as what it supposed to be.

Importance of keeping track

Some may argue why need to keep the journal when you can write them down in your memory. They should understand that the memory is just as big enough to remember the certain things not everything.

Record the journal is really important and many businesses were failing because they don't keep track on what going and will happen in their business. They just focus on the priority things or important information which are not enough.

Journal is important. However, sometimes it can be useless by the utilization of the person who record on it. The numbers on the record is just a number with no soul. If you just look on that and wonder what is wrong with the business, it will not help. When you record, make sure at least you understand why and purpose of this gain or loss number in your journal. That will be way better.

The brokers often keep the journals for the traders. However, the traders should keep their own separate journals because that is still traders' business. Traders will have more deep information and knowledge about their trades which are gain most profit or which are loss need to pay more attention.

Trade journal is

It record all of the trades from smallest to largest. In the plain reporting statement, you will now see how the trader is but in the trade journal, you will see the wide and deep information about trading. A lot of things beside numbers such as how the trader react to the trade, how the trader analysis when the market go up and down. The believe and feelings are in each trade.

The psychology of the trader is also make the journal really valuable. Each trader look at the same information in the different lens. It will show it best in the journal. That makes the forex trading really interesting from each trader. Specific character is really important in trade nowadays.

The journal is always a good reference. When the things get complicated in trade, the traders can reference their own journal to avoid the big loss or foolish or just in the moment trade. The discipline of the traders will be higher. They will have the best reminder that the time they try to deviate from their record and rules. They will give more thought and analysis to give the best decision.

Journal and trader

The relationship between journal and successful trader is really tight. The more success of the business owners, the more they keep their journal close and exact what reflect their business. As a trader, it is no exceptional with the journal too.

Trade journal is also the reason many inexperienced traders are lack to achieve the level of the experienced traders. The excellent traders always know to keep the journal in check with them all the time to see reference back to the numbers and also their feelings in the previous trades. The journal also help the traders remember more clearly when they win big and keep it going or when the loss occur happen to adjust and improve.

Improvement with journal

The good techniques and strategies can help you success in the short term. However, the fear will caught up with the winnings. Psychology is important when you trade. The journal will show the traders the best traits or the weaknesses that will help the traders improve a lot. The mental toughness of traders will be stronger with the journal record. The journal will always recall what was happened and why it happened.

Improvement is not just happen with in the trade, the journal also keep what the traders think before and after the trade, how they was feeling, what was the situation for that trade to happen and achieve that outcome. Those information are so valuable.

Traders may be uncomfortable to write on their journals, but remember the journal is completely privacy and the whole purpose to serve the traders who record their information on. Traders have no needs to show for anybody except improve themselves.

The journal with all of the things are recorded will give the specific picture for the traders, enforce the strengths, and minimize the weaknesses. The traders will be more consistent in trading. The behavior will go to the positive side which completely help the traders reach the goals easier.

Traders can count on the journal

Traders have to make our own decisions. The traders will have to live with their own decisions even the decisions are good or bad. The traders are their own boss when they make the trading. The journal will help them reflect and give the decisions which they believe is right.

Every decision is crucial and it needs to record carefully. The traders is the owner of their business. Things need to be analyzed and recorded. They cannot have the attitude things will figure it out or do it later.

In the forex industry, many people still want to blame things which are not in their favors instead they should record and keep track of what they did and why this happens to them such as the big loss in the business.

The journal will show every detail and track record. The decision which the traders make will be more appropriate and toward the winning goal. The traders will play by their own way to win instead of just blaming other people and the circumstances. Excuses are never the good solutions for business especially in trading.

Recording the good and the bad in the journal is so effective. It helps the trader not only avoiding other factors instead they will focus more on themselves. The will have the critical feedback to improve better. The detailed reference will enforce them to do better.

Useful outlining elements in journal

The traders may outline their journals in the different ways. However, the elements in most of the journals which are very similar than people think it is.

These are includes: the condition of the market at that time. It is very important to record the market condition to future reference. Then time which when the trade was happened. Next is the exchange rate which is so important in forex.

Next is recording how big of the trade. The size of the trade to help manage the capital to put in and manage the money more effective. The final is the outcome. How the trade was going, what the traders achieve, and what the traders can do better next time. The whole reflect about the trade.

These are just the most common things in the journal. The traders will be the one to decide at the end what more need to be put in the journal. The more details are always needed.

Provide truths for the journal

Everything of the trade was happened should also go in the journal. Certain traders just select what they want to put in the journal, and what they do not want to put in. You need to put all of the truths in the journal.

The journal is really the awesome feedback for the traders see what strategies was work and produce the best results for them. The traders also can eliminate what strategies was useless or inappropriate with their trade.

The traders will have the comprehensive feed back about themselves with the journal. This is at some aspects will be more value than the statistics number and so on. The reason behind is that the traders have the full reflect and see what the did and value their actions after all.

Traders can either record the journal in their computer or the electronic chart. However, many traders like the traditional way of write it down in the notebook because they feel it more comfortable.

Reference the journal before trading

Traders should always open the journal before start to make a trade transaction. It will help them more confident and jot the memory back to what happened with the last trades. The thought process of the last trade was good or not. That is a good reminder to have next to the traders to avoid repeat silly mistakes and frustration.

If the market is moving quick, the traders think they need to jump in quick to get the good profit. They will make the spontaneous or at the moment decision without any reference, and that is always happened with the loss and frustration after the trade. That is the human nature of completely don't want to miss out on the trending upwards.

However, the traders look at the journal and realize that this mistake was also happening before. This opportunity is completely not good for me. It will make the action of the traders more rationally. This action here is only the huge step to reach to success and benefit their trading career.

Many experienced traders is saved by their journals. The bad experience in the past become the useful tool for not even the present but also the future. They avoid the big loss or the awful trap and make the rational trade to win bigger. They also establish their positions higher and more experience in the trading world.

That is the big reason why a lot of new traders in this field wonder that how the experienced traders know when to jump in, open their position, extent the stay, close the trade at certain point even the trade still looks quite profit. The journal is the big reason that those decisions was made. The experienced traders assess their journals very certain and careful. Any detail is a gold indicator for success. The journal really help the traders keep track of anything they need for future use from trader's character, behavior when trading to the helpful alert mistakes which can cost the trader a huge fortune.

The forex journal can be a mentor and also the best buddy for the traders. The journal have the perfect percent of logical system because it is backed up by facts, data and all of records even in the smallest points. No software or memory can give the traders the best record like the journal do.

The outside factors can affect the traders with the emotional decisions. Emotion decisions are very dangerous in trading because the traders will get caught up in the moment. The journal just grab them with the realistic information and put them in the right way.

When the traders encounter with the big chart and data of the market in forex, the journal can be counted on all the time. It gives the traders the nice view about their experience. It enforce the best qualities of the the traders and alert the mistakes to avoid completely. The traders will keep improving in each and every trade.

The journal will help the fear or doubt about failure go away because the traders have the strong backup data about what they did. When they wake up in the morning, review the journal before jumping to the charts of trading. Hit-or-miss is never the option when they consult with their best buddy journal.

In forex trading, discipline guideline is very important. It will help avoid the randomness actions. Many people fail because the first couple mistakes from randomness actions was treated with careless. However, day by day it will add up and create a fixed bad habits. Journal keep the traders discipline which things they should do and which things they should not do. Experienced traders always watch their journal again before every trade. They knew that the more they do that the more close to perfect decisions that they will make.

Just imagine instead of spending a lot of money to learn the lessons in trading. traders get the best experience with strengths, weaknesses and strategies in your own recording book. It was next to them all the time within a hand reaching.

Break down and apply from the journal

The journal provide the good past information about the way that the traders do with forex. The clear picture is always there. The traders will get the value refresh with no cost. They will reflect to see if they follow their plans exactly. Understanding exactly when to make the reasonable entrance and stay in the market with the right strategies of trading and discipline character.

Reference with the journal in every trade. When you trade, you will have different ways such as using your personal strategies, system strategies or sometime you just let the trade run automatic. Reference and analyze with the journal to collaborate the techniques together. You should always ask questions and wonder how improve it better. You should never forget to record after that.

The traders should always analysis what they did, and how it affects on the established principles in their journal. If they deviate, they will see the results. The results may be not well, traders should fix that back to the principles. The results may be better sometimes, the traders should record to improve and update for the journal. The traders should always in check with their emotional state when trading. The decisions need to be relying on the facts and effective strategies and the experienced record from the journal.

Typical software to run the journal

The trading journal nowadays is running on software also. It will have the same benefits to analyzing the behavior of the traders. The journal software is either free or purchase and available on the market. Besides that, some traders actually computer savvy and they go on and build their own software for their own journal recording.

One of the popular software is Excel of Microsoft. It is used not only by forex traders but very popular in the trading world in general. Traders can create the spreadsheet of what they want include in the journal or they can buy the already made form. The other one is the websites that the developers create to open publicly for use or charge fee. The traders have to post their data up to the software to analyze.

Purchasing software from the developers can range between $99 to under $200 depend on how many markets that the traders want to follow in the market. Most of the software will track all of the metrics in the journal such as how many time did the traders trade, profit, loss, frequency, average loss, average profit, expectancy and so much more. These are the completely system of keep track on your journal of trading.

Many traders prefer online or websites access. Many creating journal websites are available with or without fee such as Tradingstats, TradeBench and so on. The users need the email address for log in information to access the websites later. These website journals will keep of the information to manage and analyze to help the traders.

Protect your own information

The traders will do most of the trading online via the internet with their computers. Protect their privacy information is the most important thing before they can think about success make a lot of money with forex trading.

One of the first suggestion is backing up your own data. Most of traders often ignore this step because it is very easy and can wait later. Traders should have another place or external hard drive to copy all of the important data. You will be surprise how many times you forget or your devices get lost.

Trader's computer should have virus and malware protection software. You should install the antivirus software for your computer. This will protect your computer from attack of the virus try to destroy or steal the important information in your computer and also trading business.

New virus will get appear in the future, that is why you should do your best to keep update your antivirus software. The software needs to make sure from the legit company because of your protection. If you are not sure where the software come from, you will not want to install that in to your devices.

Related to antivirus software, traders may also need the firewall software. The computers which they purchase often have firewall included. If the device did not have it, you should just install the firewall. This is the good way for the device to avoid and block strange or harm information try to access to it. You need to regularly update the firewall also.

In any account, you must have the strong and secure password. Password is so important these days. Password is not even online in your trading account but general accounts that you have via the internet.

The password needs to be long, combine with numbers, uppercase characters, lowercase case characters and also the special characters. Traders cannot use their password related to their birthdays, phone number, home address, pet names and such as. The hackers will try to capture the account if the password is too simple.

Traders also need to decide for themselves in certain period like couple months that they will have to update the new password. Sticking with one password for a long time is not a smart choice especially with the professional trader. The last thing we want is that some hackers completely stole our accounts.

The account password is only belong to you. You are the only can access your trading account. You should not share your account with anybody because it will bring the high risk of get hacked or losing your account.

Trader should have their own devices or computers. If you use public devices, you will run into high risk of somebody tracking your private information. You also need to aware of information when you send out or receive an email. You should never include the private information on the emails.

Chapter 4: Making the perfect plan to trade

The experienced traders always focus to make and write down the plan before trading. The plan is important, and it is the map to start exploring the forex trading world. However, many traders completely ignore the plan. We plan anything to do day by day routine, then also when we come to the trade, it needs to be pay attention.

When we plan for the trade, we have the intentions to create the principles and rules for us to trade wisely. It is never feeling good if we break the rules in any aspect of life. We will get in trouble. If we break the rules in our trading ways, it will not be good either.

Forex trading plan is

Trading plan is the main part of what you trade. This is your rules and principles of what you want to do in each transactions. You will describe clearly, sum up the way you trade, preparation before the trade, how you trade and what do you feel after the trade.

The trading plan should not wordy and long. It should clearly and short for the trader to easy to follow and make the right decision. Some argue that if the longer the plan the better. It is not totally true.

The trader's time is value, there will the big chance that the trader will not stop and read the plan before trading if it was 20 pages long. That really seems like too much work for time value environment of forex trading.

Another mistake that traders have is that they never want to change the plan when they process in their trading career. You should always open minded and improve the plan at the same time you progress in your career.

Revision the plan is so key. Keep update and improve your experience in your plan. It will take a little bit of time from you. However, it will keep you update with your skills and the constantly changing environment of forex.

Essential of planning

Every business always has a plan to operate that business to and achieve to the highest level either in revenue, profit, customer service or any other aspects. Trading is needed to look with the eyes of the business too.

You cannot treat forex trading just like the hobby that whenever I want I will do it. It will never work. The plan is need to be written down to the traders who are running their trading business with high disciplines. The disciplines that the plan provides will make the business run well and progress toward the goals.

The traders are the head of their trading business. They operate their own business, and nobody has the right to tell them what to do. They can do what they think on the forex market. However, the risk will be really high.

The plan is the rule book for the trader to follow whenever they need to make a trade. The traders can always test the plan when they trade in the market and get the value lesson what is working and what is not. Then the update plan will serve better purposes in the future.

Starting the plan

Everything needs a start so do the plan. Traders should always focus on starting the plan before any trade happens. Different traders will have different way to start. As long as they start to plan, everything will be useful.

The plan of action is needed to be at first. The strategies are the fundamental roads to win and achieve the goals that the traders set. You will need to write many details for each strategies. The details help creating the defined strategy.

The market conditions are important also. What is the good market conditions, what is not the good ones. How it will happen if the trade start in this market condition. The details are put in the plan.

In the plan, you should first pick the time that you plan to trade and the time that you exit the trade. The time needed to be pick clearly and that is work best for you and your trading conditions. You cannot just jump in and out whenever you want. That is not good because for awhile, you will not sure what you are doing on the market.

The plan can include 10 to 20 currency pairs to get your attention. The plan will get updated more when the traders progress. The currency pairs will also get updated. It depends on your time frame such as weekly bi weekly and so on that you set. The currency pairs may be more or lesser.

Planning with strategies on your trading plan helps you have a strong mental readiness. Everyday you wake up that will not the same like last day. Some nights you have a good nights but some nights you have worries about the market. That is why the trading plan and the strong mental readiness will help you develop your skills and move forward smoothly. If you feel not ready for the trade because of the mental preparation, it will be better to postpone a bit, look the plan and relaxing yourself before give the final decision.

Know the risk in trading

The traders should define the risk in their trading plan. It depends on the traders to how much risk they can bear and handle. The standard is 2% risk per trade. Some can bear higher, some can bear lower.

In addition, the traders should also include the money value they decide to risk. Some traders can bear for about $100 risk of losing per trade. The number of money is also the defined factor for traders do the trade. The combination will help a lot with the exact number the traders want to risk without the fear of trading appear.

Return and reward

The risk is one of the good fact to measure the trade. In addition, the experienced traders also focus on the return or what they will get reward for the trade. The reward is the money that the traders will get.

The reward is calculated with the ratio. The reward ratio is what the traders set up. It will be different from low to high by different traders. For example, the traders will risk $10 and if profit is $40. The reward ratio is 4 time. This number is always mentioned like a important factor for traders.

Plan to enter and exit the market

The traders need to define the fit and best plan for them to enter the market. What is the conditions of the market, what is the methods they will use and other factors. This is the important step for traders.

Planning to exit the market is crucial too. When the traders plan their strategies, they often forget when they will need to exit the market. Planning to exit the market is really benefit when you know that you want to exit to stop the loss. Then when you want to exit because you make enough the profit and achieve your goal n the trade.

What to do after the trade

The experienced traders always focus on the after trade even they earn profit or take a loss. The important thing is the traders will get the useful feedback and good take away key points. There are the big potential mistakes that the traders will make after the trade.

Some traders just want to jump back to the market right away to win back what they lost in the last trade without planning. The risk is really high. Some traders will feel too confident without need to consult their strategies. The risk is also high in this case. The after trade information is the best updated for the trading plan.

Chapter 5: Tools for mastering forex trading

In any business, the tools are really crucial to how the business operate. In forex trading, this is as well similar situation. The new traders or the experienced traders need the tools to master their trade and also make the right decisions to reach their goals.

Nowadays the trading tools can be with fee or without fee. Many platforms offer free trading tools for traders to use in the basic level. Some platforms offer the subscription. Traders become the members and pay the services monthly or yearly.

Economic calendar

The economic calendar is helping the traders get the fresh and updated news such as what happen in the future of the market, important related to trading economic data, new policies from the central bank, the elections and monetary policies updated around the world and much more. These are really important for trading especially forex market.

You can get the economic calendar from brokers or financial websites. It will provide the big picture about the economy such as the events that impact the economy in what level, unemployment rate, expecting the market conditions. Traders will have to keep close eyes on these things because trading currencies will be effective.

The level of impact in each event will be effective the economy. The currency pair will get effective as well. The market volatility of forex trade will be either low or medium or high depends on the events.

Pip calculator

Pip is the measure unit, and it is the most popular and smallest measure unit in forex trading especially between the currency pair. The pip calculate is convenient to use. Many traders use this forex trading tool to easy in exchange the pair currency. The users just have to enter the detail of their position, the amount of the currency, size of trade, currency pair and also the leverage.

Time zone converter

Forex market has 3 biggest markets around the world. One market closes, then another market open. That is why some traders can trade 24 hours. Besides that, the market also overlap with each other so the traders can also trade 2 markets at the same time.

With the right strategies, traders can get double profit. Time zone converter helps traders know exactly which market is opening in exactly what time. The experienced traders often trade around 3 or 4 morning Eastern time because they can trade in London market which is the biggest market for forex. It also overlap with the Asia forex market.

Volatility calculator

Traders should focus and always keep eyes on the market volatility. It can help you have the good view about which is a good currency pairs to choose for trading. You do not want the currency pairs with limited scope of volatility because it will not the best trade.

Volatility calculator will give the general the history exchange of these currency pairs, and give you the overall of how much volatility the pairs will be. You will decide if you want to trade on those pairs or not.

The history exchange can help the user pick what is the time frame that they want to focus on week, month, quarter or even years. The more market volatility is the better chance for traders to make the profit.

The traders can see the time frame with the currency pairs yield the most return, and they can start to trade on that time frame when it comes. It is working both ways that high return will also be high risk included. The traders can manage to diversify the trading to protect the money by risk management strategies.

Currency correlation

Forex trading is all about currency pairs. Traders is be sure to not ignore the correlation between the currency pairs. The easy way to signal the currency pairs correlation is mark them positive or negative correlation.

The correlations range from -1.0 to 0.0 to +1.0. These are easy to understand: -1.0 is the perfect negative or inverse that often marked with color red color, 0.0 is no correlation, +1.0 is the perfect positive that often marked with blue.

The correlations between of currency pairs are calculating based on the history data between them. One of the popular currency correlation tool that many traders are known of is Mataf. Besides, You can also search and will see a lot of online websites offering this tool for free.

Trading platform

Many trading platforms are available nowadays. The most used platform by experienced trader is MetaTrader 4. The feature of this platform is one of the best and comprehensive in the market. MetaTrader 4 has a strong analysis functions. The chart is really clear and easy to understand. Traders can put in currency pairs directly to the chart to comparing the up and down of the market.

MetaTrader 4 has a lot of advantages. Many traders use it, so if you run into the problems, you can easily to find the right answer quickly. MetaTrader 4 can operate and link with other software. Users can run automated trading with this platform smoothly.

MetaTrader 4 is not only using for forex trade but also using for different types of trading such as stocks, bonds, gold and much more. Traders can download MetaTrader 4 on its online website. They can try, test their data. This platform is really for the serious traders.

Chapter 6: Choosing currencies to trade

The strategies or method for trading is necessary. However, the traders need to know how to pick what currency pairs to trade. If you pick the wrong what you want to trade, you will not make profit even you have the perfect strategies in the world.

Each currency is representing for primary of each economy. When you trade for currency pair, you need to have to collect and understand two different economies and how these two economies related in may aspects. They will be complex also.

New traders should just focus on the currency pairs have steadiness and decent spreads. The liquidity is also important. The volatility is needed but only the new traders can proactively participate. These are essential keys to pick the currency pairs for trading if you are new to forex market.

Currency pairs

As we known, the basic of forex market is buying and selling currencies. Trading is always by pair of currencies. We have base currency and the other side is counter currency. We need to know the information of how much the exchange rate.

For example, EUR/USD has the quote 1.24. That means 1 EUR is worth $1.24. EUR is base currency. USD is counter currency. That is how forex market works. The currency pair is necessary to form for the traders to do transaction. These are some prominent currency pairs that traders always focus on.

Euro and US dollar

Euro and US dollar are two of the biggest currencies in the world. People often think about the exchange rate between Euro and US dollar even though they are not the forex trader. That is said forex traders are often do a lot trading with these currencies.

The liquidity of these two currencies are large. They are really stable. The spread is low because the large trade of these two currencies is happened often. The traders can be easy to track and use strategies on trading these two. With the new traders, these are the most recommended currency pair.

US dollar and Japanese yen

USD/JPY is also the powerful currency pair. New traders can learn really fast about volatility of forex market if they trade with this currency pair. This currency pair is very liquid, and the new traders should not put too much money before they have more experience in hands.

The JPY is usually up and down by certain time frame and patterns. The USD is more stable by time. Traders can see the patterns of this currency pair and make good benefit in trading. Commodities trading is related strongly to JPY.

New traders should keep close eyes on commodity price. Natural disasters and politics also make JPY market very volatility. The traders are advised to leave the currency pair because of high volatility and unpredictable at these time. Besides that, JPY is very strong related to Asia market. This is one of the factors to explain for its volatility.

British Pound and US dollar

GBP/USD is one of the most heard of currency pair. This currency pair is fair and easily to predict. These two economies are very stable. The currency pair is really a good field for new traders to put their money in. It is the oldest currency pair of forex market.

GBP/USD and EUR/USA are strong related in trading market. Traders often like to trade the two currency pairs to more secure for their trade. They are similar so it will give more security than the big gain profit.

US dollar and Canadian dollar

This currency pair is good to take look at also. These two currencies is effective and doing well with commodities. The ways that these two is running are very similar economy. Besides that, they have some different characters that traders can clearly see.

The oil industry in United States is one of the most different point between the two economies. It cause some volatility between the two currencies, and the traders can take advantages with good strategies at these given time.

This currency pair is profit enough for new traders and also the experienced traders because of the stability between the two countries. However, traders should keep update because some changing politics issues can cause the big volatility.

Australian dollar and US dollar

USD is the most popular in the trading world. The Australian dollar is strong currency and attract a lot of traders also. They make AUD/USD is the attractive currency pair in the forex market.

The new traders and experienced traders always interest in Australia economy. Its economy has a stable growth for many years. That will be easy to predict the growth of Australian dollar. The volatility is also giving the traders many specific gain.

The choice

All the good choice in forex market often include the US dollar because it is the most popular currency in the world. It is still go strong and stable. When traders do the it to pair with other currencies, it will give them more benefit.

The traders should also watch out for the factors such as economy, political issues and so on in any currency. The right strategies are necessary too because you trade with the two currencies with the different economies.

Chapter 7: Common terminologies in forex trading

Ask price - what market accept that currency at minimum price.

Aussie - this is Australian dollar.

Base currency - the first currency is based on the quote between the currency pair.

Bid price - The maximum price the market will buy the currency.

Blind entry - trading to the market without look for the signal.

Cable - the nickname of the GBP/USA back then years ago.

Candlestick - one of the popular price action method.

Exchange rate - the price of one currency to another currency when they are exchanging.

Forex charts - the chart show how forex market and traders can see what spots are good or trade.

Spread - the different between bid and ask price. Bid price subtract ask price.

Symbol - the short way to write any country's currency.

Chapter 8: Traits of successful forex traders

Successful forex traders often have these traits in common. These traits are not only natural but traders can cultivate over period of time. There are always chances for traders to improve and better at what they are doing

Discipline in trading

Discipline is applying for any single aspects in life. If you want to success, you have to be discipline to what you do every time. Forex traders need discipline to give the right decisions in their career. It will help lead them go to the right path and avoid a lot of pitfalls.

Passion about what we do

Passion is really needed in the forex trading world. Passion is the fuel that help the traders stick and move forward to achieve their goal. Many new traders gave up too soon because they come with just the expectation but without passion. This trait is one of the most important to become a successful trader.

Willing to do whatever it takes

When you first start trading, you will encounter in many difficult situations. You may also fail a lot of times. Some will give up easily because it is too hard for them. You will have to do what it takes to keep moving forward and achieve your goals. With that purpose, you will cancel a lot of negative feelings.

Be Patient

As a new trader, you should be patient. You will have to spend a lot of time to learn new skill, set up the effective strategies, test and may be fail time to time. The patience helps you know that you are not ready yet and you need to full preparing before you make a trade. It also helps you avoid a lot of costly mistake. The experienced traders are the ones that are really patient in their professional career.

Develop a wining habit

When you are new a career, you will encounter many difficult issues. You will learn a lot of value lesson. In life, you are for sure have many habits. In your trading career, habit is also important. You will cultivate a winning habit if you decide you want to be successful.

Always learning and staying up to date

The forex trading is constantly updated with the new thing every day. As a trader, you should keep your information updated such as reading news, watching financial news and so on. You should make sure that you understand what is going on in your career. Besides that, you should keep learning the new things or software to see how it can adapt in your daily strategies of trading.

Conclusion

Thank you for making it through to the end of this book. I hope the information in this book will be helpful for you. The forex trading is always an interesting world to get in because it has a lot of potential to grow for both new traders and experienced traders.

www.ingramcontent.com/pod-product-compliance
Lightning Source LLC
Chambersburg PA
CBHW030055230526
45471CB00003B/1112